CONTENTS:

Copyright notice:
Practice Paper 1: Extract from *The Woman in Black* by Susan Hill, published by Vintage Books ©
Susan Hill 1983. Reproduced by permission of Sheil Land Associates Ltd.

INTRODUCTION:

Hello! Thank you for buying this pack of practice papers. If you're at this point, you must be getting ready for your English language exams, so we have a few words of advice for you:

1. Exams aren't bad. They're your opportunity to show off just how much you know about English—and you have been studying it since you were five, so you definitely know a thing or two! Don't worry about your exams—worry never changes anything—instead, try and see them as an opportunity to show off what you know.
2. Practising exam papers is a good way to revise and, because this exam is still relatively new, there aren't that many past papers out there. The papers in this book have been created to try and replicate the exam experience for you. Some people might suggest using your literature texts for practice, but the whole point of this exam is that it is unseen: it's best to work on extracts you've never read before.
3. There is more than one way to tackle an exam paper. You could sit it in one go and complete it in exam conditions from start to finish. You could go at the papers gently, with modelled examples in front of you to help (check out the videos at youtube.com/mrbruff). Another method is to try three question threes all in a row, slide tackling your way through the paper. You might want to complete all of the Section B questions before beginning Section A. However you do it, take your time, and use the indicative content at the end to check your work.
4. The indicative content isn't everything. You might make a point that we haven't included. Marking your own work is quite difficult so, although these are good to practise on, you should share with someone who understands the marking system to mark your work and give you feedback.
5. This book is not a guide to the exam: it is a set of practice papers. For a detailed question-by-question guide to AQA English language, you should pick up a copy of 'Mr Bruff's Guide to GCSE English Language' in paperback on Amazon, or eBook at mrbruff.com.

Please note: we are not endorsed by or affiliated to the AQA exam board. We are simply two experienced teachers creating resources.

FREE GIFT: The eBook edition of this book contains colour images. You deserve those too, so email info@mrbruff.com with proof of purchase, and we will email you the eBook edition for free.

Source A:

In this extract, taken from the mid-point of a novel, the narrator witnesses a dangerous situation whilst walking across a causeway (a road which regularly floods).

1 For a short time, I walked slowly on, determined to stick to my path until I came out onto the safety of the country road. But it began to dawn on me that I should as likely as not become very quickly lost once I had left the straightness of the causeway, and might wander all night in exhaustion. The most obvious and sensible course was to turn and retrace my steps the few hundred yards I had
5 come and to wait at the house until either the mist cleared, or Keckwick arrived to fetch me, or both.

That walk back was a nightmare. I was obliged to go step by slow step, for fear of veering off onto the marsh, and then into the rising water. If I looked up or around me, I was at once baffled by the moving, shifting mist, and so on I stumbled, praying to reach the house, which was farther away
10 than I had imagined. Then, somewhere away in the swirling mist and dark, I heard the sound that lifted my heart, the distant but unmistakable clip-clop of the pony's hooves and the rumble and creak of the trap. So Keckwick was unperturbed by the mist, quite used to traveling through the lanes and across the causeway in darkness, and I stopped and waited to see a lantern—for surely he must carry one—and half wondered whether to shout and make my presence known, in case he
15 came suddenly upon me and ran me down into the ditch.

Then I realized that the mist played tricks with sound as well as sight, for not only did the noise of the trap stay further away from me for longer than I might have expected but also it seemed to come not from directly behind me, straight down the causeway path, but instead to be away to my right, out on the marsh. I tried to work out the direction of the wind but there was none. I turned around
20 but then the sound began to recede further away again. Baffled, I stood and waited, straining to listen through the mist. What I heard next chilled and horrified me, even though I could neither understand nor account for it. The noise of the pony trap grew fainter and then stopped abruptly and away on the marsh was a curious draining, sucking, churning sound, which went on, together with the shrill neighing and whinnying of a horse in panic, and then I heard another cry, a shout, a
25 terrified sobbing—it was hard to decipher—but with horror I realized that it came from a child, a young child. I stood absolutely helpless in the mist that clouded me and everything from my sight, almost weeping in an agony of fear and frustration, and I knew that I was hearing, beyond any doubt, appalling last noises of a pony and trap, carrying a child in it, as well as whatever adult— presumably Keckwick—was driving and was even now struggling desperately. It had somehow lost
30 the causeway path and fallen into the marshes and was being dragged under by the quicksand and the pull of the incoming tide.

I began to yell until I thought my lungs would burst, and then to run forward, but then stopped, for I could see nothing and what use would that be? I could not get onto the marsh and even if I could there was no chance of my finding the pony trap or of helping its occupants, I would only, in all
35 likelihood, risk being sucked into the marsh myself. The only thing was to get back to Eel Marsh House, to light every light and somehow try and signal with them from the windows, hoping against all reason that this would be seen, like a lightship*, by someone, somewhere, in the countryside around.

Shuddering at the dreadful thoughts racing through my mind and the pictures I could not help but
40 see of those poor creatures being slowly choked and drowned to death in mud and water, I forgot my own fears and nervous imaginings of a few minutes earlier and concentrated on getting back to the house as quickly and safely as I could. The water was now lapping very close to the edges of the path though I could only hear it, the mist was still so thick and darkness had completely fallen, and it was with a gasp of relief that I felt the turf and then the gravel beneath my feet and fumbled my
45 way blindly to the door of the house.

Behind me, out on the marshes, all was still and silent; save for that movement of the water, the pony and trap might never have existed.

* lightship - a boat using a light to warn or guide those at sea

Section A: Reading

Answer **all** questions in this section.
You are advised to spend about 45 minutes on this section.

01 Read again the first part of the source, from **lines 1 to 6**.

   List **four** things about the narrator and his surroundings from this part of the source.   **[4 marks]**

1 _____

_____

2 _____

_____

3 _____

_____

4 _____

_____

02 Look in detail at this extract from **lines 7 to 15** of the source:

That walk back was a nightmare. I was obliged to go step by slow step, for fear of veering off onto the marsh, and then into the rising water. If I looked up or around me, I was at once baffled by the moving, shifting mist, and so on I stumbled, praying to reach the house, which was farther away than I had imagined. Then, somewhere away in the swirling mist and dark, I heard the sound that lifted my heart, the distant but unmistakable clip-clop of the pony's hooves and the rumble and creak of the trap. So Keckwick was unperturbed by the mist, quite used to traveling through the lanes and across the causeway in darkness, and I stopped and waited to see a lantern—for surely he must carry one—and half wondered whether to shout and make my presence known, in case he came suddenly upon me and ran me down into the ditch.

How does the writer use language here to describe the narrator's journey?

You could include the writer's choice of:

- words and phrases

- language features and techniques

- sentence forms.   **[8 marks]**

_____

_____

_____

_____

_____

_____

_____

_____

_____

_____

_____

_____

03 You now need to think about the **whole** of the Source. This text is from the middle of a novel.

How has the writer structured the text to interest you as a reader?

You could write about:

- what the writer focuses your attention on at the beginning of the source

- how and why the writer changes this focus as the source develops

- any other structural features that interest you.   **[8 marks]**

04 Focus this part of your answer on the second half of the source, from **line 16 to the end**.

A student, having read this section of the text said: ,This extract shows how confused the narrator feels. It makes the reader feel the same way'.

To what extent do you agree?

In your response, you could:

- Write about your own impressions of the narrator
- Evaluate how the writer has created these impressions
- Support your opinions with quotations from the text. **[20 marks]**

_____

_____

_____

_____

_____

_____

_____

_____

_____

_____

_____

_____

_____

_____

_____

Section B: Writing

You are advised to spend about 45 minutes on this section.
You are reminded of the need to plan your answer.
You should leave enough time to check your work at the end.

05 A travel website is running a creative writing competition.

Either:

Write a story based on this picture:

Or

Describe a time you went somewhere you'd never been before.

(24 marks for content and organisation and 16 marks for technical accuracy)   **[40 marks]**

Source A:

> Using chemicals, an art restorer returns damaged paintings to their original condition in order to preserve the artwork. Philip Harper is working in his studio, when he is paid a visit by an art dealer who asks him to do something illegal.

1 The canvas had yellowed. Varnish that had at one point protected and secured the artwork, had now switched allegiances, and its once proud shine had dulled to an opaque cloud. The art restorer sat in front of the canvas, the date 1589 still visible in the upper left hand corner, and inhaled slowly. He was ready to remove the lacquer∗.

5 At first, liquid forms in small spools on the surface of the canvas, and then the brush goes to work. It delicately churns and twists in the solvent. In that moment a small battle takes place: the invasion of yellow and brown has been ejected by the insurgent∗ solvent. The art restorer's white gloved hand takes the cotton swab and sweeps in tiny precise movements, lifting the old varnish from the painting entirely. Then there, naked underneath, is the bright skin of the cheek of an Elizabethan
10 noblewoman. More liquid, and more swirling, and more lifting; soon the inch square is complete. And then the next square is started. Only another one thousand seven hundred and twenty seven inches to go.

Outside the studio, there was a small sign: 'Philip Harper, Conservation and Art Restoration, est.1962'. Next to the sign there was a buzzer. A black gloved hand pushed its thumb down on the
15 buzzer and held it there, lifted it, and then pressed again. Inside the studio, Philip jolted slightly at the sudden noise, placed down his brush and swab. "One minute, one minute," he muttered.

Before Philip had a chance to pull the door fully open, the black glove shoved it open, and two people pushed into the studio. Attached to the black glove was a black clothed body. The body had a head, topped with a black fedora, and feet inside heavy black boots. Behind him was a smaller and
20 rather more colourful figure. A woman, dressed in flamboyant colours, with a small bejewelled turban upon her head.

"What can I do- " Philip was interrupted almost immediately.
"You are an art restorer. I am an art dealer. You are going to look at this painting. I am going to tell you to replicate it. You will object- but I warn you now, it would be wise not to bother." The
25 woman snapped out the sentences crisply, and held her left arm outstretched. Her accomplice placed in her hand a black tube.

Philip began to object, "I'm very sorry madam, but you seem to have misunderstood. I restore paintings, I don't offer a reproduction service, that isn't my area at- "

Again, he wasn't allowed to finish his sentence.

30 "This painting here," the woman gestured towards her accomplice, who obligingly held up a photograph, "is a forgery. You painted it. It's a good forgery, and you fooled me- but you now have a choice. You can either paint me a forgery, just like you did for Signora de la Cruz, or you can be reported to the authorities, and never work again."

Philip's lips formed an O shape, but no words came out. Instead, his left hand went to his forehead,
35 and his right hand to his chin, and quivered there for a half minute while he composed his thoughts.

His head dropped, and he seemed to be studying the floor, as if somewhere on the carpet there was an answer to this horrible mess of a dilemma.

Last July, Philip had received a message from an old friend, a fellow art restorer. She had been working on an ancient Dutch Master. It had been x-rayed, and her team were certain that there had
40 been discolouration of the skin tone, and to the background. However, once work had begun, it quickly transpired that there was no discolouration here. The colours became too bright, too harsh. Instead of resembling the gloomy day intended by the artist, it looked as if there was bright sunshine streaming through the trees, and the sky had turned a cartoonish blue.

Philip had rushed to his friend's side. She was in a fury- tearing down the photographs and x rays,
45 and kicking over chairs, and hurling paintbrushes at the wall. From a drawer she pulled a pistol. She was going to be ruined- her career would become nothing more than a joke, her life would be over. Philip had to calm her.

And so they made a plan. He would paint a copy, and with all the attention on the restoration, they would be able to pass it off as the original. No one would know. Her team would think she'd
50 corrected the error. Disaster would be averted. The pistol was put away. As Philip began to consider the enormity of what he'd agreed to, a small frisson* shivered over him: he would be a criminal. This was a crime.

And so Philip painted. Long into the night, he painted. His eyes were sore and red and bloodshot, from peering at his canvas, and the original, and the dozens of photographs pinned around the easel.
55 And then it was finished.

In the weeks that passed, Philip hardly slept, his mind whirred in a constant state of panic and anxiety, convinced that his crime had been uncovered. His friend stopped replying to his messages, telling him he needed to 'get a grip'. Alone with his guilt, Philip returned to his normal work. He only felt the smallest glimpse of reassurance when the grand unveiling of the newly restored
60 painting passed with hardly a mention in the local press.

And now this. Philip looked up from the floor; he wasn't a tall man, but in that moment he looked grey and small, as if somebody had turned the saturation down in a photograph. When he nodded, it was an almost imperceptible wobble of his chin.

"Excellent," smirked the woman. "Now, let's take a look at what we're working with."

* lacquer- a liquid that dries to form a protective coating
* frisson- a sudden powerful feeling of fear or excitement
* insurgent- a rebel fighting against an invading enemy or government

Section A: Reading

Answer **all** questions in this section.
You are advised to spend about 45 minutes on this section.

01 Read again the first part of the source, from **lines 1 to 4**.

List **four** things about the painting from this part of the source. **[4 marks]**

1 _____

_____

2 _____

_____

3 _____

_____

4 _____

_____

02 Look in detail at this extract, from **lines 5 to 12** of the source:

At first, liquid forms in small spools on the surface of the canvas, and then the brush goes to work. It delicately churns and twists in the solvent. In that moment a small battle takes place: the invasion of yellow and brown has been ejected by the insurgent solvent. The art restorer's white gloved hand takes the cotton swab and sweeps in tiny precise movements, lifting the old varnish from the painting entirely. Then there, naked underneath, is the bright skin of the cheek of an Elizabethan noblewoman. More liquid, and more swirling, and more lifting; soon the inch square is complete. And then the next square is started. Only another one thousand seven hundred and twenty seven inches to go.

How does the writer use language here to describe the process of restoring the painting?

You could include the writer's choice of:

• words and phrases

• language features and techniques

• sentence forms. **[8 marks]**

_____

_____

_____

_____

_____

_____

_____

_____

_____

_____

_____

03 You now need to think about the **whole** of the source.

This text is from the beginning of a short story.

How has the writer structured the text to interest you as a reader? You could write about:

- what the writer focuses your attention on at the beginning of the source

- how and why the writer changes this focus as the source develops

- any other structural features that interest you.   **[8 marks]**

_____

_____

_____

_____

_____

_____

_____

_____

_____

_____

_____

_____

_____

_____

_____

_____

_____

04 Focus this part of your answer on the second part of the source, from **line 38 to the end**.

A student said, 'This part of the story, where Philip is remembering when he forged the painting, shows Philip was actually not to blame for the forgery, and he has been taken advantage of.'

To what extent do you agree?

In your response, you could:

- consider your own impressions of who was to blame

- evaluate how the writer conveys Philip's situation

- support your response with references to the text.   **[20 marks]**

Section B: Writing

You are advised to spend about 45 minutes on this section.
You are reminded of the need to plan your answer.
You should leave enough time to check your work at the end.

05 A magazine has asked for contributions for their creative writing section.

Either:

Write a description of this room as suggested by this picture:

or

Write a story about a time when a visitor arrives unexpectedly.

(24 marks for content and organisation and 16 marks for technical accuracy)   **[40 marks]**

This source comes from the beginning of a novel. Lucian Taylor attends boarding school, and is home for the holidays.

1 The holidays were nearly done, and Lucian Taylor had gone out resolved to lose himself, to discover strange hills and panoramas that he had never seen before. The air was still, breathless, exhausted after heavy rain, and the clouds looked as if they had been moulded of lead. No breeze blew upon the hill, and down in the well of the valley not a dry leaf stirred, not a bough* shook in
5 all the dark January woods.

About a mile from the rectory he had diverged from the main road by an opening that promised mystery and adventure. It was an old neglected lane, little more than a ditch, worn ten feet deep by its winter waters, and shadowed by great untrimmed hedges, densely woven together. On each side were dark streams, and here and there a torrent of water gushed down the banks, flooding the lane.
10 It was so deep and dark that he could not get a glimpse of the country through which he was passing, but the way went down and down to some unconnected hollow. Amid the dead and wearied silence of the air, beneath leaden and motionless clouds, it was strange to hear such a tumult of gurgling and rushing water, and he stood for a while on the quivering footbridge and watched the rush of dead wood and torn branches and wisps of straw, all hurrying madly past him,
15 to plunge into the heaped spume*, the barmy froth that had gathered against a fallen tree.

When he got home he heard his mother's voice calling: "Here's Lucian at last. Mary, Master Lucian has come, you can get the tea ready." He told a long tale of his adventures, and felt somewhat disappointed when his father seemed perfectly acquainted with the whole course of the lane, and knew the names of the wild woods through which he had passed in awe.

20 "You must have gone by the Darren lane, I suppose"—that was all he said. "Yes, I noticed the sunset; we shall have some stormy weather. I don't expect to see many in church tomorrow."

There was buttered toast for tea "because it was holidays." The red curtains were drawn, and a bright fire was burning, and there was the old familiar furniture, a little shabby, but charming from association. It was much pleasanter than the cold and squalid schoolroom; and much better to be
25 reading the newspaper than learning Algebra; and better to talk to his father and mother than to be answering such remarks as: "I say, Taylor, I've torn my trousers; how much do you charge for mending?" "Lucy, dear, come quick and sew this button on my shirt."

That night the storm woke him, and he groped with his hands amongst the bedclothes, and sat up, shuddering, not knowing where he was. He had seen himself, in a dream, within the Roman fort,
30 working some dark horror, and the furnace doors were opened and a blast of flame from heaven was smitten upon him.

Lucian went slowly, but not without academic recognition, through the years at the school; gaining prizes now and again, and falling in love more and more with useless reading and unlikely knowledge. He knew his Shakespearean poetry well enough, but he preferred exercising himself in
35 the rhymed Latin of the middle ages. He liked history, but he loved to think about a land laid waste, Britain deserted by the legions, the rare pavements riven by frost, Celtic magic still brooding on the wild hills and in the black depths of the forest, the rosy marbles stained with rain, and the walls growing grey.

The masters did not encourage these researches; a pure enthusiasm, they felt, should be for cricket
40 and football, the *dilettanti** might even play fives and read Shakespeare without blame, but healthy English boys should have nothing to do with decadent periods.

He was once found guilty of recommending Villon, whose autobiographical poems describing his criminal exploits gave Lucian much enjoyment, to a school-fellow named Barnes. Barnes tried to extract unpleasantness from the text during prep class, and rioted in his place, owing to his inability
45

to appreciate the language. The matter was a serious one; the headmaster had never heard of Villon, and the culprit gave up the name of his literary admirer without remorse.

Hence, sorrow for Lucian, and complete immunity for the miserable illiterate Barnes, who resolved to confine his researches to the Old Testament, a book which the headmaster knew well. As for Lucian, he plodded on, learning his work decently, and sometimes doing very creditable Latin and
50 Greek prose. His school-fellows thought him quite mad, and tolerated him, and indeed were very kind to him in their barbarous manner.

Lucian often consoled himself by thinking about how in after life acts of generosity and good nature done by wretches like Barnes, who had no care for old French nor for curious poems, and such thoughts always moved him to happiness. Travellers tell such tales; cast upon cruel shores amongst
55 savage races, where they have found no little kindness and warmth of hospitality.

* bough - the branch of a tree
* spume - foam or froth
* *dilettanti* - Italian for 'amateur'

Answer **all** questions in this section.
You are advised to spend about 45 minutes on this section.

01 Read again the first part of the source, from **lines 1 to 5**.

List **four** things about the setting from this part of the source.   **[4 marks]**

1 _____

_____

2 _____

_____

3 _____

_____

4 _____

_____

02 Look in detail at this extract, from **lines 6 to 15** of the source:

> About a mile from the rectory he had diverged from the main road by an opening that promised mystery and adventure. It was an old neglected lane, little more than a ditch, worn ten feet deep by its winter waters, and shadowed by great untrimmed hedges, densely woven together. On each side were dark streams, and here and there a torrent of water gushed down the banks, flooding the lane. It was so deep and dark that he could not get a glimpse of the country through which he was passing, but the way went down and down to some unconnected hollow. Amid the dead and wearied silence of the air, beneath leaden and motionless clouds, it was strange to hear such a tumult of gurgling and rushing water, and he stood for a while on the quivering footbridge and watched the rush of dead wood and torn branches and wisps of straw, all hurrying madly past him, to plunge into the heaped spume, the barmy froth that had gathered against a fallen tree.

How does the writer use language here to describe the countryside?

You could include the writer's choice of:

- words and phrases

- language features and techniques

- sentence forms.   **[8 marks]**

03 You now need to think about the **whole** of the source.

This text is from the beginning of a novel.

How has the writer structured the text to interest you as a reader? You could write about:

- what the writer focuses your attention on at the beginning of the source

- how and why the writer changes this focus as the source develops

- any other structural features that interest you.   **[8 marks]**

04 Focus this part of your answer on the second part of the source, from **line 32 to the end**.

A student said, 'This part of the story, where Lucian is thinking about his time at school, shows how alone Lucian feels, and he has no one who understands him.'

To what extent do you agree?

In your response, you could:

- consider your own impressions of who was to blame

- evaluate how the writer conveys Lucian's situation

- support your response with references to the text.   **[20 marks]**

_____

_____

_____

_____

_____

_____

_____

_____

_____

_____

_____

_____

_____

_____

Section B: Writing

You are advised to spend about 45 minutes on this section.
You are reminded of the need to plan your answer.
You should leave enough time to check your work at the end.

05 A competition for writing stories is being held online, and you have decided to enter.

Either:

Write a story of a journey as suggested by this picture:

or

Write a story about a time when a person felt isolated or alone.

(24 marks for content and organisation and 16 marks for technical accuracy)   **[40 marks]**

Source A:

> This source comes from the middle of a novel. Sammy has murdered his friend Frankie, and has now taken on his identity. A police inspector has called to say he wants to speak to Frankie, so Sammy is preparing to speak to the officer, whilst pretending to be Frankie.

1   It was when I was stood at my balcony that a thought occurred to me: after two years of travelling around the continent, I had come to a conclusion that Italian afternoons last longer than afternoons in any other country in Europe. The sun lingers, and the streets are warmer, and the people sleepier. Venetian afternoons last the longest of all. Those tourists who plagued the beaches of the Riviera all
5   summer, are now diminished in number, and have headed to Venice; in the afternoons you can find them lolling about in gondolas, or snapping photographs near the Rialto whilst misquoting Shakespeare.

From the moment I ended the telephone call to Inspector Bianco, I had known I was safe. I knew and I was certain; I had absolutely no doubt in my mind. All the buzzing thoughts in my head
10 cleared- like mist on a mirror in a steamy bathroom- fizzing away and leaving you with your own reflection looking back. The Inspector wasn't hauling me in for questioning- they were popping by for a chat! A chat! A little chat and a glass of whisky, no doubt. Because we know what these Italian Polizia are like, don't we? Fools. Incompetents. If they hadn't found the motorcycle with the bent mirror, or the blood stained clothes, or the skull of Francis Beaumont III bashed in with a
15 rock...well, then they had nothing.

Now, I'm not cold hearted, please don't think I didn't feel sad for what happened to poor Francis- of course, I had wept, wept for hours, but at that point, I needed to turn my attention to the room. I narrowed my eyes and surveyed my pitiful den where I'd been hiding out for the last month. The room was hazy from the stale smoke, and it hung close to the ceiling. I realised I needed this room
20 to appear unequivocally* to belong to Frankie, and I would need to make sure any traces of Sammy were gone.

And so I roamed between the two rooms of the apartment, viewing it now through the eyes of a policeman: was this the apartment of an eligible bachelor from New York? Had I left out some clue that would betray me as an imposter? Prowling the tiles in the bathroom I got into character. Like
25 an actor in the wings, awaiting his cue to stride on and deliver his lines, ready to strut and peacock and woo the audience. I felt ready.

Although I'd been up for hours, I hadn't yet dressed myself, and so I dug around in Frankie's suitcase for his monogrammed tie, and his pinkie ring. Jamming it onto my finger, I started to practice his voice again, and pulled on one of Frankie's winter shirts, and a pair of chinos.

30 "Oh, awfully sorry, old chap, to have caused you such a fuss," I looked into the mirror hanging over the bathroom sink. I then said it again, elongating the vowel sounds, until they rounded and rolled like Frankie's. "A motorbike? Oh yes, we hired a motorbike. Spot of bother when we returned it. A motorbike? Oh yes, we got a motorbike."

The lines repeated again and again, until the story was straight in my head. Sorry for the fuss. A
35 motorbike? Yes, we had an accident. Caught my hand when I came off at a turn. Healed mostly now. Yes, Sammy went back home, or to Austria- he always talked about Austria. No, no idea where he is. I'm staying on here and working. Playing the piano. Earning enough to get by. Yes, I wrote those cheques. That's my signature. Here's my passport. Here's a letter from my mother. Awfully sorry for the fuss.

40 From the mantle piece came the reproachful* 'tick tick' of the clock. I shaved, and ran my fingers through my strawberry blonde hair, cocking my chin to the side as Frankie was known to. 'Ever so good of you to come, Inspector. Bianco? Isn't it?' I practiced again and again, my whole mind had
45 become a razor, and I was carving away at myself until the shape of Frankie was there, and Sammy was extinguished. The more I said it, the more I began to feel like Frankie again, and the more relaxed I became. I've never been one for vanity, but I did take a moment to congratulate myself on the believability of my performance.

I walked out onto the balcony and looked down over the piazza. School boys weaved in and out of the slow moving crowds with footballs tucked under their arms, and ladies rested the arms of their parasols on their shoulders, and everything seemed to move in a glorious harmony.

50 And in that gorgeous sunshine, I spotted the distinct uniform of a policeman, accompanied by a tallish Italian with a purposeful gait. Ah ha, I thought to myself, this is our Inspector. And then, I felt something rupture in my stomach, and the air escaped my lungs in a long drawn out hiss of disbelief. For there, two steps behind, strode my mother.

* unequivocally - in a way that leaves no doubt
* reproachful - expressing disappointment or disapproval

Section A: Reading

Answer **all** questions in this section.
You are advised to spend about 45 minutes on this section.

01 Read again the first part of the source, from **lines 1 to 7**.

List **four** things about Venice from this part of the source. **[4 marks]**

1 _____

_____

2 _____

_____

3 _____

_____

4 _____

_____

02 Look in detail at this extract, from **lines 8 to 15** of the source:

> From the moment I ended the telephone call to Inspector Bianco, I had known I was safe. I knew, I was certain, I had absolutely no doubt in my mind. All the buzzing thoughts in my head cleared- like mist on a mirror in a steamy bathroom- fizzing away and leaving you with your own reflection looking back. The Inspector wasn't hauling me in for questioning- they were popping by for a chat! A chat! A little chat and a glass of whisky, no doubt. Because we know what these Italian Polizia are like, don't we? Fools. Incompetents. If they hadn't found the motorcycle with the bent mirror, or the blood stained clothes, or the skull of Francis Beaumont III bashed in with a rock…well, then they had nothing.

How does the writer use language here to describe how the narrator felt after the phone call from the Inspector?

You could include the writer's choice of:

• words and phrases

• language features and techniques

• sentence forms.   **[8 marks]**

_____

_____

_____

_____

_____

_____

_____

_____

_____

_____

_____

_____

03 You now need to think about the **whole** of the source.

This text is from the middle of a novel.

How has the writer structured the text to interest you as a reader?

You could write about:

- what the writer focuses your attention on at the beginning of the source

- how and why the writer changes this focus as the source develops

- any other structural features that interest you. **[8 marks]**

_____

_____

_____

_____

_____

_____

_____

_____

_____

_____

_____

_____

_____

_____

_____

_____

04 Focus this part of your answer on the second part of the source, from **line 22 to the end**.

A student said, 'This part of the story, where Sammy is preparing to trick the detective into thinking he is Frankie, shows that he was too focussed on trying to impersonate his friend, and was therefore unprepared to see the detective arrive with his mother.'

To what extent do you agree?

In your response, you could:

- consider your own impressions of who was to blame

- evaluate how the writer conveys Sammie's situation

- support your response with references to the text.   **[20 marks]**

_____

_____

_____

_____

_____

_____

_____

_____

_____

_____

_____

_____

_____

_____

_____

Section B: Writing

You are advised to spend about 45 minutes on this section.
You are reminded of the need to plan your answer.
You should leave enough time to check your work at the end.

05 | Your local newspaper is running a creative writing competition.

Either:

Write a description of a day in a city, as suggested by this picture:

or

Write a story about a time when there is a case of mistaken identity.

(24 marks for content and organisation and 16 marks for technical accuracy)   **[40 marks]**

Source A:

> Septimus Smith and his wife Lucrezia are part of a crowd in a busy London street which is captivated by a passing car supposedly containing an important traveler.

1   Septimus Warren Smith, aged about thirty, pale-faced, beak-nosed, wearing brown shoes and a shabby overcoat, with hazel eyes which had that look of apprehension in them which makes complete strangers apprehensive too. He looked at things that others did not see; he spoke to people who were no longer with him. Although he had left the army, and the war was over, there were
5   remnants∗ of the war that had not left him. He stood outside the florist, whilst his wife was inside choosing flowers.

Everything had come to a standstill. The throb of the motor engines sounded like a pulse irregularly drumming through an entire body. The motor car had stopped outside Mulberry's shop window; old ladies on the tops of omnibuses spread their black parasols; here a green, here a red parasol opened
10   with a little pop. Mrs. Dalloway, coming to the window with her arms full of sweet peas, looked out with her little pink face pursed in enquiry. Every one looked at the motor car: Septimus looked; boys on bicycles sprang off; traffic accumulated. And there the motor car stood, with drawn blinds. Septimus thought- this gradual drawing together of everything to one centre before his eyes, as if some horror had come almost to the surface and was about to burst into flames, terrified him. The
15   world wavered and quivered and threatened to burst into flames.

'It is I who is blocking the way,' he thought. Why was he being looked at and pointed at? Why was he weighted there, rooted to the pavement? For a purpose? But for what purpose?

"Let us go on, Septimus," said his wife Lucrezia. She was a little woman, with large eyes in a sallow∗ pointed face; an Italian girl.

20   But Septimus could not help looking at the motor car and the tree pattern on the blinds. Was it the Queen in there—the Queen going shopping?

"Come on," said Lucrezia. But Septimus jumped, started, and said, "All right!" angrily, as if she had interrupted him. People must notice; people must see. People, she thought, looking at the crowd staring at the motor car; the English people, with their children and their horses and their clothes,
25   which she admired in a way. Suppose they had heard him? She looked at the crowd. Help, help! she wanted to cry out to butchers' boys and women.

Help! Only last autumn she and Septimus had stood on the Embankment wrapped in the same cloak. But failure one conceals. She must take him away into some park.

"Now we will cross," she said. She had a right to his arm, though it was without feeling. He would
30   give her (she who was so simple, so impulsive, only twenty-four, without friends in England, who had left Italy for his sake) a piece of bone.

The motor car with its blinds drawn and an air of inscrutable seriousness proceeded towards Piccadilly, still gazed at, still turning the faces on both sides of the street with the same dark breath of veneration whether for Queen, Prince, or Prime Minister nobody knew. Whispers in the crowd
35   said the face itself had been seen only once by three people for a few seconds.

But there could be no doubt that greatness was seated within; greatness was passing, hidden, down Bond Street, removed only by an arm's length from ordinary people who might now, for the first and last time, be within speaking distance of the majesty of England. So close to the enduring symbol of the state which will be known to historians of the future, sifting the ruins of time, when
40 London is a grass-grown path and all those hurrying along the pavement this Wednesday morning are but bones and teeth and gold rings in the ground. The face in the motor car will still be known.

It is probably the Queen, thought Mrs. Dalloway. And for a second she wore a look of extreme dignity standing by the flower shop in the sunlight while the car passed at a foot's pace, with its blinds drawn.

45 The car passed slowly through the busy street, and then disappeared, but it had left a slight ripple which flowed through glove shops and hat shops and tailors' shops on both sides of Bond Street. For thirty seconds all heads were inclined the same way—to the window.

* remnants - a small remaining part of something
* sallow - yellow or pale brown complexion

Answer **all** questions in this section.
You are advised to spend about 45 minutes on this section.

01 Read again the first part of the source, from **lines 1 to 6**.

List **four** things about Septimus Warren Smith from this part of the source.   **[4 marks]**

1 _____

_____

2 _____

_____

3 _____

_____

4 _____

_____

02 Look in detail at this extract, from **lines 7 to 15** of the source:

Everything had come to a standstill. The throb of the motor engines sounded like a pulse irregularly drumming through an entire body. The motor car had stopped outside Mulberry's shop window; old ladies on the tops of omnibuses spread their black parasols; here a green, here a red parasol opened with a little pop. Mrs. Dalloway, coming to the window with her arms full of sweet peas, looked out with her little pink face pursed in enquiry. Every one looked at the motor car: Septimus looked; boys on bicycles sprang off; traffic accumulated. And there the motor car stood, with drawn blinds. Septimus thought- this gradual drawing together of everything to one centre before his eyes, as if some horror had come almost to the surface and was about to burst into flames, terrified him. The world wavered and quivered and threatened to burst into flames.

How does the writer use language here to describe the reaction to the car?

You could include the writer's choice of:

• words and phrases

• language features and techniques

• sentence forms. **[8 marks]**

_____

_____

_____

_____

_____

_____

_____

_____

_____

_____

_____

_____

03 You now need to think about the **whole** of the source.

This text is from the beginning of a short story.

How has the writer structured the text to interest you as a reader?

You could write about:

- what the writer focuses your attention on at the beginning of the source

- how and why the writer changes this focus as the source develops

- any other structural features that interest you.   **[8 marks]**

_____

_____

_____

_____

_____

_____

_____

_____

_____

_____

_____

_____

_____

_____

_____

_____

04 Focus this part of your answer on the second part of the source, from **line 20 to the end**.

A student said, 'This part of the story, where Lucrezia is watching the reaction to the car, shows how unhappy she is about her life, and her relationship with Septimus.'

To what extent do you agree?

In your response, you could:

- consider your own impressions of who was to blame

- evaluate how the writer conveys Lucrezia's situation

- support your response with references to the text.   **[20 marks]**

You are advised to spend about 45 minutes on this section.
You are reminded of the need to plan your answer.
You should leave enough time to check your work at the end.

05 A website has asked for contributions for their creative writing section.

Either:

Write a description of this scene as suggested by this picture:

or

Write a story about a time when two people feel unhappy together, who have previously been happy.

(24 marks for content and organisation and 16 marks for technical accuracy)   **[40 marks]**

Source A:

> This source comes from the middle of a novel. In the last month, the city has had an infestation of rats, and the mayor, Abraham, took Mr Vogel (a stranger to the city) up on his offer to rid the town of the rats. Mr Vogel has delivered on his promise, and has now arrived at Abraham's office to give Abraham his invoice and collect his payment for the service.

1   Inside Abraham's office the light was bright, and the afternoon sun shone in through the large floor to ceiling windows that filled the entire back wall. His view overlooked the city, with the river a dark ribbon of green snaking through the sky scrapers. Instead of positioning his office furniture to maximise this grand panorama, Abraham had his mahogany table and leather chair facing the door,
5   and a plain brown wall. His walls were bare apart from one wall hanging: an oil portrait of Abraham himself, in full mayoral robes.

Mr Vogel stood waiting in the office for Abraham to arrive, and in his hand he clutched a sheet of paper. He hovered halfway between the powerful door and the desk, feeling like a schoolboy sent to see the headteacher, and now trying to remember which piece of homework he'd copied off a
10   friend. The room was filled with a clawing silence, and Vogel itched to fill it with sound to somehow reassure himself that he was actually there, and it wasn't just a strange dream. On the desk a small clock ticked out the seconds, dividing the time neatly into minuscule chunks, and the seconds slipped to minutes, which grew to an hour. Still Vogel waited.

With a grunt of frustration, the door swung open, and thudded against the wall. Abraham strode in
15   without looking at Vogel, and dropped his black leather briefcase onto the desk with a heavy thud of self importance. Across his forehead there was a sheen of sweat, and his hand pawed at his pocket to find a handkerchief to mop up his perspiration. Although he was barely much more than forty, his face belonged to a man much older: his nose was purple from broken blood vessels; his teeth had been stained brown from coffee and then red from wine, resulting in a dentures the colour
20   of sludge; beneath his eyes there were two dark circles, and his proud chin disappeared into the jowls of his neck.

Abraham's eyes moved to the mahogany desk, and Vogel's invoice: payment required for services provided; number of rats estimated at 200,000; fee includes the disposal of the rats. The number on the bottom matched the one that Abraham had bragged he would pay- back at the first whole town
25   meeting. Mr Vogel stood next to the table, and with one finger he pushed it towards Abraham, who was sat in his chair.

"You can't have thought I was serious?" laughed Abraham. As he lent back in his chair, his jacket fell back, and his shirt stretched over his expansive stomach. "I can't actually believe you've brought me this, you- is this a joke? Am I meant to laugh?"

30   If Abraham's words worried Vogel, he wasn't going to let him know it. Vogel kept quiet, and let Abraham rattle on, the sneers and insults rolling off him, as if the mayor was critiquing some separate and unrelated thing: the last football match he'd watched, or a poor quality takeaway he'd just eaten.

"On the invoice it states it must be paid within 14 days. Your promptness is appreciated, as I would
35   like to leave town before the weather changes," Vogel's voice remained level and steady.

"You'll be waiting a lot longer than fourteen days, my boy, a lot longer, because, because, because besides, we never signed a contract! I never signed a thing, if-if-if you wanted to be paid, y'know, you should have got a contract drawn up, a-a-and, you didn't." Abraham's face was turning puce, and his words wavered up and down the octaves, as if he was impersonating an opera singer.

40 Instead of arguing back, Vogel gave a little nod, and gestured towards the contentious piece of paper, still resting on the desk like a stick of unexploded dynamite. He turned and left the room, but before he closed the door, he pulled back, and looked Abraham full in the face.

"I'll collect payment, one way or another, so if I were you, I'd pay it."

And with that he closed the door.

45 Abraham's body that had been tense and stiff throughout the whole encounter, now relaxed, and he bent over slightly as air escaped in one long sigh of relief. Shaking himself slightly, he took out his handkerchief again, and gave his face one last mop over, before clicking open his briefcase. He started to sift through the papers, but his mind wouldn't focus, and in frustration he jabbed at the desk, knocking the papers everywhere, and the invoice shot off the edge and floated to the ground.

50 Irritated and perturbed*, Abraham wheeled his chair round and looked out and down over the city. Beneath, he watched as a pick up truck towed away a car that had been left abandoned at the side of the road, the tyres gnawed away by the now absent rats.

The rats. His breakfast, without the rats, was immensely better than what it had been. As was his commute, as was his morning briefing, as was his daily update on the news coverage. Hamelin was
55 immeasurably improved now Vogel had rid them of the rodents.

But they were broke! 'Even if I wanted to pay him, I couldn't!' Abraham told himself. He rolled the lie round in his thoughts and then said it aloud: "I want to pay him, of course! We just can't afford it!".

He smiled. Satisfied with how it sounded, he turned back to his desk and re-shuffled his papers, and
60 commenced his work. He didn't stop to pick up the invoice, and when he left that evening, he walked out of the office, leaving it lying on the floor.

* perturbed - feeling unsettled or anxious.

Section A: Reading

Answer **all** questions in this section.
You are advised to spend about 45 minutes on this section.

01 | Read again the first part of the source, from **lines 1 to 6**.

List **four** things about the office from this part of the source. **[4 marks]**

1 _____

_____

2 _____

_____

3 _____

_____

4 _____

_____

02 Look in detail at this extract, from **lines 7 to 13** of the source:

Mr Vogel stood waiting in the office for Abraham to arrive. He hovered half way between the powerful door and the desk, feeling like a schoolboy sent to see the headteacher, and now trying to remember which piece of homework he'd copied off a friend. The room was filled with a clawing silence, and Vogel itched to fill it with sound to somehow reassure himself that he was actually there, and it wasn't just a strange dream. On the desk a small clock ticked out the seconds, dividing the time neatly into minuscule chunks, and the seconds slipped to minutes, which grew to an hour. Still Vogel waited.

How does the writer use language here to describe the time Vogel spends waiting in the office?

You could include the writer's choice of:

• words and phrases

• language features and techniques

• sentence forms. **[8 marks]**

03 You now need to think about the **whole** of the source.

This text is from the middle of a novel.

How has the writer structured the text to interest you as a reader?

You could write about:

• what the writer focuses your attention on at the beginning of the source

• how and why the writer changes this focus as the source develops

• any other structural features that interest you.   **[8 marks]**

04 Focus this part of your answer on the second part of the source, from **line 45 to the end**.

A student said, 'This part of the story, when Abraham is left alone in the office, shows that Abraham enjoys feeling powerful, and has been put on edge by his conversation with Vogel.'

To what extent do you agree?

In your response, you could:

- consider your own impressions of who was to blame

- evaluate how the writer conveys Abraham's situation

- support your response with references to the text.   **[20 marks]**

_____

_____

_____

_____

_____

_____

_____

_____

_____

_____

_____

_____

_____

_____

_____

_____

Section B: Writing

You are advised to spend about 45 minutes on this section.
You are reminded of the need to plan your answer.
You should leave enough time to check your work at the end.

05 | Your local council is running a creative writing competition and they plan to publish the winning entry.

Either:

Write a story based on this picture:

> **or**

Write a story titled 'Rubbish'

(24 marks for content and organisation and 16 marks for technical accuracy)   **[40 marks]**

INDICATIVE CONTENT – PRACTICE PAPER 1

QUESTION 1:

CREDIT: He walked slowly / He was determined to stick to his path / He was on a causeway / It was misty / He was heading for the country road / He thought he might become lost

DO NOT CREDIT: He was lost / He was exhausted

QUESTION 2:

AO2 content may include the effect of:

'nightmare' use of metaphor to reflect the difficulty involved, foreshadowing difficulties ahead

'praying to reach the house' use of religious language, links to the supernatural

'clip-clop' use of onomatopoeia, lack of full sensory description creates sense of mystery

'mist' use of pathetic fallacy creates sense of mystery and horror

'veering / rising /moving / shifting' use of verb choices to emphasise the uncertainty of the journey

QUESTION 3:

- The text opens by establishing a clear sense of time and place and the reader is lulled into a false sense of security. It seems like an ordinary journey but will soon become supernatural / horrifying

- Continual shift and change between mental state and setting creates sense of confusion and chaos

- Repetition of references to 'mist' emphasise inescapable situation for the narrator

-Ambiguity of final clause reinforces sense of mystery, 'save for that movement of the water, the pony and trap might never have existed.'

QUESTION 4:

-Use of first person narrator, 'I', ensures reader is as confused as narrator

-Use of primarily sound imagery, 'clip-clop', without accompanying visual imagery, suggests confusion

-Use of rhetorical question, 'what use would that be?' suggests confusion

-Pathetic fallacy of 'mist' symbolises confusion

-Semantic field of confusion, 'tricks / baffled / curious / hard to decipher'

QUESTION 1:

CREDIT: The painting had yellowed / The painting had been varnished / The painting varnish had dulled to an opaque cloud / The painting was dated 1589 / The painting was going to be restored / The painting was now not as clear as it used to be / The painting had discoloured / The painting needed to be restored / An art restorer was going to fix the painting / The painting was on canvas / The painting had been varnished to protect it

DO NOT CREDIT: The painting was Elizabethan / The painting was of a noble woman / The painting had solvent put on it

QUESTION 2: AO2 content may include the effect of:

'The brush goes to work' use of personification suggesting the difficulty involved and how the brush comes to life- almost magical

'small battle' use of oxymoron, metaphor to reflect the complexity and difficulty in what he is doing

'Only another…' use of hyperbole, irony, the idea it is complex and time consuming, painstaking, requires patience

'more liquid…' the repetition of 'more' to emphasise the complexity of the task

QUESTION 3: A02 content may include the effect of:

- Begins with the legitimate work of art restoration, and ends with him agreeing to forge the painting. Signifies how greatly his life has changed, and emphasises the difference turn his life has taken - change in fortune - past catching up on him.
- painting is 'yellowed' and at the end Philip is 'grey and small'- both Philip and the painting have been effected by external forces / pressures / events / time.
- flashback to back story of Philip - creates a complex character - poses his dilemma - explains why the action of the first third of the story took place.
- contrast of Philip to the art dealer - Philip seems vulnerable and weak, whereas the art dealer is assertive and strong.

QUESTION 4:

-Philip came up with the plan with his friend- 'we came up with a plan' -suggests he was compliant/agreed to it

-Philip found the idea exciting 'frisson of excitement'

-Philip does find his job dull 'only another…'

-He only did it because his friend's behaviour was escalating 'tearing down the photographs and x rays, and kicking over chairs, and hurling paintbrushes at the wall.'

-Philip felt compelled to do something to stop her using the gun 'He had to do something'

INDICATIVE CONTENT – PRACTICE PAPER 3

QUESTION 1:

CREDIT:The air was still / There were clouds in the sky / It had been raining / It was January / There were leaves in the valley

DO NOT CREDIT: Lucian felt sad (anything to do with feelings- not setting) / Lucian enjoyed being on his own/had no friends / Lucian was on holiday

QUESTION 2: AO2 content may include the effect of:

'old neglected', use of adjectives to create negative impression

'densely woven together', used to create sense of mystery

'dark streams' 'deep and dark', use of colour imagery to create a sense of the unknown

'dead and wearied' emotive language used to create ominous tone

'leaden and motionless clouds', pathetic fallacy

QUESTION 3: A02 content may include the effect of:

-Flashback in paragraph two 'About a mile from the rectory he had' - reflection on the bike ride that symbolises his further isolation

-Shift from narrative to dialogue in paragraph three - the dialogue illustrates how his inner isolation is then further compounded by his father's distance

-Chronological jump in paragraph six, 'That night the storm woke him' the storm symbolises his awakening/anger

-Flashback, 'He was once found guilty of recommending Villon' -signifies how his history has formed his future

QUESTION 4:

-Negative language used to describe his love of reading and knowledge, 'useless reading', 'unlikely knowledge'

-Imagery of loneliness, 'laid waste / deserted' symbolises isolation felt by Lucian

-Negative language choices, 'found guilty', reflects Lucian's feeling of not being understood

-His father does try and speak to him/he does have friends - dialogue flashbacks

-'His school-fellows thought him quite mad, and tolerated him, and indeed were very kind to him in their barbarous manner.' - triple, the many ways his friends were good to him

QUESTION 1:

CREDIT: They are sunny/the sun lingers / The streets are warm/it is warm / The afternoons last the longest(in Europe)/longer / It is full of tourists / The tourists go on gondolas / The tourists take photographs near the Rialto / The tourists have come from the beaches and go to Venice / The people are sleepy

QUESTION 2: AO2 content may include the effect of:

'absolutely no doubt' - superlative, level of certainty - confidence - over confident - level of arrogance - considers himself to be smarter than the police etc

'like mist in a mirror clearing' -simile - suggests sudden realization, symbolises how this clarity lets him see his own situation more clearly

'hauling' vs 'popping' - serious vs causal contrast - indicates the easy time he will have - how he sees himself as being safe now

'if if if'- conditional clauses - the level of incompetence of the police, and the level of criminality of Sammy

QUESTION 3: A02 content may include the effect of:

-At the beginning he is confident, but by the end he is totally unravelled – in between his confidence was growing, and he was behaving in a morally reprehensible way (wearing his dead friend's clothes and planning his deception for the police) there is satisfaction to think he will get caught by the Inspector he called 'incompetent'

-Unreliable narrator - he is a murderer, a liar and a thief - we don't trust what he says, and his claims that 'I've never been one for vanity' seems ridiculous given what we know

-Information is staggered/dripped out, we hear about what happened with Frankie bit by bit

-The story is a memory- perspective of someone looking back on the action 'from that moment' suggests that this moment was a crucial turning point in his life, and that the events here have impacted him forever

-Everything takes place in the room - claustrophobic - feel the pressure that Sammy does as he awaits the interview

QUESTION 4:

-'I practiced again and again, my whole mind had become a razor, and I was carving away at myself until the shape of Frankie was there, and Sammy was extinguished.' metaphor - that Sammy was too focussed on his impression

-'Had I left out some clue that would betray me as an imposter? Prowling the tiles in the bathroom I got into character.' hypophora/rhetorical question - being self questioning, he was trying to prepare for other outcomes - but focus wasn't on his mother turning up

-'The more I said it, the more I began to feel like Frankie again, and the more relaxed I became.' repetition of 'more' overconfidence, misguiding, lets guard down

INDICATIVE CONTENT – PRACTICE PAPER 5

QUESTION 1:

CREDIT: He was thirty/pale faced/beak nosed/wearing brown shoes/shabby overcoat/hazel eyes /
He looked apprehensive /and he made others felt apprehensive too / He looked at things others didn't see/spoke to people who were no longer with him / He left the army / There were parts of the war that had not left him /

DO NOT CREDIT: He was still in the army

QUESTION 2: AO2 content may include the effect of:

Simile, 'sounded like a pulse' creates imagery of the car being alive

Short sentence, 'Everything had come to a standstill' reflects intensity of the moment

Sensory imagery, 'throb of the motor engines' sense of importance - mirroring the excitement of the onlookers

Personification, 'there the motor car stood', highlights the allure of the vehicle

Personification / hyperbole, 'The world wavered and quivered and threatened to burst into flames.' highlights the exaggerated reaction to the car.

'everything' 'everyone' superlative - the draw of the car captures everyone

QUESTION 3: AO2 content may include the effect of

-Opening focus is on Septimus, leading the reader to favour him over Lucrezia

-Shift from character description to action in paragraphs 1-2. Septimus' internal thoughts, together with the previous description of character, now provide the reader with a fully rounded character

-Shift from narrow focus of character description in paragraph, 1 zooming out to show a panoramic view of the busy London setting highlights the isolation Septimus feels and why he feels the way he does

-Shift in line 22 from previous thoughts to dialogue between Septimus and Lucrezia widens the scope of the text and adds increased tension

-Flashback, 'Only last autumn she and Septimus' creates sympathy for both characters, and intrigue as to what has caused the relationship to suffer

QUESTION 4:

- 'for a second she wore a look of extreme dignity', temporary nature of happiness

-Flashback, 'Only last autumn she and Septimus', suggests that past was happier

-Short exclamatory sentence, 'Help!' suggests that present time is unhappy

-Short, monosyllabic communication with Septimus, "Come on" and "Now we will cross" suggests lack of communication between the couple and reflects unhappiness

-Repetition of 'people': 'People must notice; people must see. People, she thought' shows how - Lucrezia is more interested in the reaction of others than that of Septimus, reflecting troubled relationship between the two

-Reference to time, 'for a second she wore a look of extreme dignity' highlights fleeting nature of happiness

INDICATIVE CONTENT – PRACTICE PAPER 6

QUESTION 1:

CREDIT: It was light / It had large windows / It overlooked the city/river/skyscrapers / The furniture faced away from the windows / It contained an oil painting of Abraham / It had a mahogany table/leather chair / It had plain brown wall

DO NOT CREDIT It was the afternoon / It was sunny

QUESTION 2: AO2 content may include the effect of:

'like a schoolboy' -simile- feels less powerful

'clawing silence' - metaphor/personification - discomfort/animalistic- not in control

'seconds-minutes-hours' time was passing and feeling oppressive - time was passing slowly

'itched' his emotional discomfort has become physical - the depths of his unhappiness at being there, predicting trouble, foreshadowing what comes later

'hovered' and 'powerful' he is out of place there, unsure where to put himself

QUESTION 3: A02 content may include the effect of:

- Vogel and Abraham are in conflict- physically contrasting characters, Abraham fits the role of villain, and Vogel the hero, but Abraham doesn't see himself as a villain

- begins and ends with the invoice- this is the focus of the story, the conflict arises from the invoice, and it stays in the room symbolising how it is still a problem, even though Vogel threw it away

- Vogel and Abraham swap positions. Vogel is alone, then joined by Abraham, and then Abraham is alone. At the beginning, it is Vogel who is uneasy, and at the end, it is Abraham who feels uneasy

-

QUESTION 4:

-" is this a joke? Am I meant to laugh?" rhetorical questions to be insulting - he knows it isn't a joke, he is trying to undermine Vogel and put him off pursuing him for the money- trying to use his power to undermine Vogel

-'Abraham's face was turning puce, and his words wavered up and down the octaves, as if he was impersonating an opera singer.' simile - shows Abraham is bothered and therefore does know Vogel has power in the situation

-The painting in the office/furniture facing away - Abraham is inward looking, enjoys feeling important, but isn't a 'good' ruler

-'He rolled the lie round in his thoughts and then said it aloud' the 'rolled' suggests he is toying with it, playing with it

Printed in Great Britain
by Amazon

56731108R00056